SPECIAL DAYS
Winter

Cath Senker

W
FRANKLIN WATTS
LONDON • SYDNEY

SPECIAL DAYS

Titles in this series:

Autumn

Spring

Summer

Winter

© 2004 Arcturus Publishing

Produced for Franklin Watts by Arcturus Publishing Ltd, 26/27 Bickels Yard,
151-153 Bermondsey Street,
London SE1 3HA.

Series concept: Alex Woolf
Editor: Liz Gogerly
Designer: Tim Mayer
Picture researcher: Shelley Noronha, Glass Onion Pictures

Published in the UK by Franklin Watts.

A CIP catalogue record for this book is available from the British Library.

ISBN 0 7496 5460 0

Printed in Italy.

Franklin Watts – the Watts Publishing Group, 96 Leonard Street, London EC2A 4XD.

Picture Acknowledgements:
AI Pix *cover* (top, middle), *cover* (bottom, left), 5, 20, 25, 26; Andes 27; Circa Photo Library 7/ John Smith
cover (bottom, left), *cover* (bottom, right),14 / William Holtby 28; Eye Ubiquitous 29; Hutchinson/ Leslie Woodhead
12; Link 9; Ann and Bury Peerless 24; Peter Sanders 4; David Silverman/ Sonia Halliday *cover* (bottom, middle), 6;
Topham *cover* (top, right), *title*, 10, 11, 13, 16, 17, 18, 19, 22, 23; World Religions Photo Library 8, 15, 21

Cover pictures (clockwise from top left): Mahashivaratri; Id ul-Adha; Epiphany;
Magha Puja; Hanukkah; Guru Gobind Singh's Birthday.

Note:
The quotations in this book are fictionalized accounts drawn from factual sources.

Contents

Note: When Muslims say the name of one of the Prophets, they say 'Peace Be Upon Him' afterwards. This is shown in Arabic as ﷺ in this book.

Brightening up the Winter

In the **northern hemisphere**, the winter months of December, January and February are cold and the days are short. Festivals brighten up the winter.

Many cultures celebrate the winter solstice on 21 December, the day with the fewest hours of daylight. All religions celebrate New Year, although at different times. At Hijrah, the Muslim New Year, people remember how the **Prophet** Muhammad ﷺ and his followers made a new start in the city of Madinah. The theme of making a new start at New Year is common to all religions.

During the Muslim New Year people gather at the Prophet's mosque in Madinah, Saudia Arabia. It was the first mosque the muslims built when they moved to Madinah.

Hans' Advent

'It's freezing cold here in December but we really enjoy Advent, the four weeks running up to Christmas. On the first Sunday, we got up at 6 a.m. and went round the nearby houses singing Christmas carols. After church, friends invited us for a coffee party. The next few weeks were spent preparing for Christmas. We made elf cut-outs and paper chains as decorations, practised carols and baked delicious cakes.'

Hans, Kapisigdlit, Greenland

These children in Melbourne, Australia, are performing Christmas carols at a Christmas concert.

Candles and light at this dark time of year are another shared theme. For instance, candles are lit during **Advent**, Christmas and Hanukkah.

This book looks at festivals during the winter months in the **northern hemisphere**. Remember that on the other side of the world – in Australia and New Zealand – it's summer then. And in **tropical** areas, such as parts of Brazil, it can be hot all year round. Note that Muslim festivals are not fixed according to the seasons. They can take place at any time of the year.

Hanukkah, December

At this Jewish festival, people remember the time long ago when their **ancestors** stood up to their Greek rulers. The rulers wanted the Jews to follow the Greek religion, worshipping many different gods. The Jewish people believed in one God alone.

The Greeks destroyed the Jews' beautiful Temple in Jerusalem. A brave group, called the Maccabees, fought the Greeks and won. When they regained their ruined temple, they lit the holy lamps once again. However, there was only enough oil for one day. By a miracle, the oil lasted for eight days. By this time, the Jews had found new supplies of oil to keep the lamps alight.

Jewish children helping to light the Hanukkah candles. It's the last night of the festival and all eight candles are alight.

Aaron's Hanukkah

'At Hanukkah mum helped me to light the candles and we put the *hanukiah* by the window for people outside to see. We ate foods cooked in oil to remember the miracle in the Temple. Dad and I made doughnuts and *latkes* – little pancakes fried in oil. Grandma and grandpa brought us Hanukkah presents and mum gave us some money. Some kids get a small present for every day of Hanukkah!'

Aaron, Melbourne, Australia

Hanukkah is a time for friends and families to gather together. Here, a cake has been decorated with the symbol of the *hanukiah*.

Jewish people remember the miracle each year at Hanukkah and celebrate their fight for freedom. They light candles in a special holder called a *hanukiah*, which has eight branches and an extra one for lighting the others. On the first night one candle is lit, and on the second night two. On the eighth and final night all eight candles shine out into the night.

7

Christmas, 25 December

A Christmas celebration outdoors in Australia, with a little Christmas tree on the table.

At Christmas, the most popular Christian holiday, people celebrate Jesus' birth. They believe he is the Son of God, who took human form to come and live among people on Earth. Through Jesus, God was able to make himself known to humankind. Most Christians celebrate Christmas on 25 December, but **Orthodox Churches** hold the festival on 6 January.

Christians look forward to Christmas with great excitement. On Christmas morning, they go to church to sing carols about Jesus' arrival in the world. At home afterwards, they exchange presents and eat a special festive meal.

James's Christmas

'Here, Christmas comes in the boiling hot summer. On Christmas Eve, we decorated a fir tree with home-made ornaments and put the presents underneath. I woke up really early on Christmas morning and put on my best clothes. At church we sang the songs we'd been practising for ages. Afterwards we had a fantastic feast with fresh roast goat, **cornmeal** porridge and bread and jam. Then all the kids played while the adults chatted.'

James, Harare, Zimbabwe

The day after Christmas Day, people in Australia, New Zealand, Canada and the UK have another holiday – Boxing Day. It comes from the British tradition of wealthy people giving gifts or money to poorer people on that day. Yet no one knows exactly what 'Boxing Day' means.

In the **southern hemisphere** and in **tropical** countries, the weather is warm at this time and celebrations are held outdoors. In Australia, people can spend Christmas on the beach!

Candles add a festive feel to this Christmas carol service in South Africa.

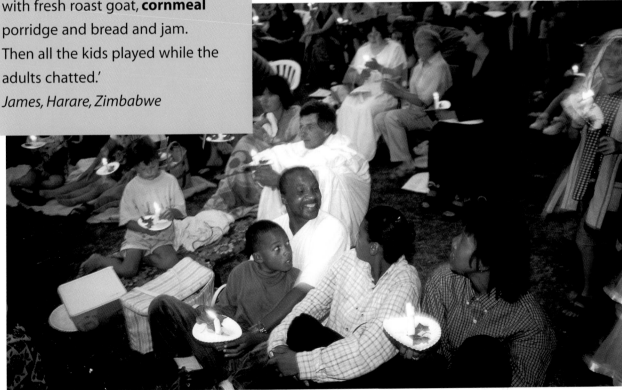

Kwanzaa, 26 December– 1 January

Kwanzaa is an **African-American** family festival, developed in the 1960s. Kwanzaa means 'first fruits' in Swahili, a language spoken in much of Africa. It reminds African-Americans that their roots are in Africa.

A family celebrating Kwanzaa at home. You can see the Kwanzaa symbols on the table.

Keisha's Kwanzaa

'This year, mum, dad and I went to a Kwanzaa party for the first time. We listened to a story about why we should celebrate. It's a festival for all African-Americans, whatever our religion. We played games, and learnt some African songs. The kids all had a turn at lighting the candles on the *kinara*. At the end, we all got a present. We're definitely coming again next year!'
Keisha, Washington DC, USA

A boy lighting the seven candles. Each one stands for one of the seven principles (the special meanings) of the festival.

Kwanzaa brings families together, and helps them to feel proud of their history and culture. Each of the seven days in the festival has a special meaning, including **unity**, supporting one another, and faith.

Every evening, people gather at home with their family and friends. The table is set with straw mats, fruits and vegetables, and ears of corn – one for each child. There are seven candles in a candle holder called a *kinara*. The three red candles stand for the blood of African people. Three green candles represent the hope of new life. The black candle is for the face of the African people.

Day six is Kuumba, meaning creativity. There is a big celebration called Karamu. People gather to enjoy a large feast. They tell folk tales from long ago and stories about great African-Americans.

New Year Celebrations, 1 January Onwards

Around the world, people mark New Year on different dates depending on their religion and traditions. Chinese New Year is in January or February. It celebrates the start of ploughing and sowing, which brings the earth back to life.

In many countries, New Year's Day on 1 January is an important festival date. It has its origins in the ancient practice of sun and fire worship in the deep midwinter. Fire ceremonies, such as torch-lit processions and lighting New Year fires, play a big part in New Year traditions. Fire is a symbol of putting the darkness of the past behind you and carrying a new light of hope into the New Year.

A young girl with dragon dancers out in the streets, celebrating the Chinese New Year.

Hamish's Hogmanay

'On Hogmanay we went to a dance called a ceilidh (you say 'kaily') at our community centre. What a laugh! Just after midnight, a neighbour came 'first-footing', with a lump of coal, shortbread, spiced cake and whisky. People used to say that if a tall, dark stranger appeared at your door like this, you'd have good luck in the New Year. Then we went visiting friends and family even though it was night-time!'
Hamish, Isle of Harris, Outer Hebrides, Scotland

The Hogmanay celebrations are in full swing in the centre of Edinburgh in Scotland.

In Scotland, New Year's Eve is called Hogmanay. In the main cities of Edinburgh and Glasgow, the celebrations start in the early evening and excitement mounts as people wait for the special moment. As the clock strikes midnight, everyone kisses each other and sings the traditional song, *Auld Lang Syne*.

Guru Gobind Singh's Birthday, 5 January

Guru Gobind Singh was the tenth and final human Sikh **Guru**. He taught the Sikhs to worship one God. The Guru said that Sikhs should be kind and help needy people in the community. It was he who introduced the Sikh 'uniform', the 5 Ks, which Sikhs always wear. They are *kangha* (comb), *kara* (steel bangle), *kesh* (uncut hair), *kachera* (shorts) and *kirpan* (small sword).

At the **gurpurb** (Guru's festival) for Guru Gobind Singh's birthday, people worship at the **gurdwara,** the Sikh temple. They take the festival outdoors with a procession. It's headed by five men, who stand for the first five people who joined the Sikh community 300 years ago. An elaborately decorated float carrying the Sikh holy book, the Guru Granth Sahib, follows the procession.

The Five Beloved Ones, representing the first five Sikhs, lead the procession carrying Sikh flags.

Guru Gobind Singh was an excellent poet and musician. In his memory, people sing his lovely hymns, accompanied by Indian instruments like the **harmonium** and **tabla drums**. Sports competitions and games are held, and young people may give displays of **martial arts**.

A display of martial arts for the festival. Sikhs believe that it is important to be strong and fit.

Kiran's *Gurpurb*

'On the day before Guru Gobind Singh's birthday, we held a large procession through the streets. All along the route people had hung banners, flags and posters about Sikhism – it looked impressive! On the Guru's birthday, mum went to the *gurdwara* at 4 a.m. for worship. Dad and I went in the evening for a shared meal of flat bread, bean stew and curry. We stayed way past my bedtime.'
Kiran, Calgary, Canada

Epiphany, 6 January

Children in church acting out the story of the Three Kings' visit to baby Jesus.

Epiphany is a Christian festival to celebrate the Three Wise Men, also known as the Three Kings. The word Epiphany means 'made known'. On this day, the newborn baby Jesus was shown to the Wise Men, who gave him precious gifts. Christians are happy that Jesus became known to many people. To mark the occasion, **Catholics** hold a special **mass** in church.

The **Orthodox Churches** celebrate Christmas on 6 January. This date is also the focus of Christmas celebrations in Latin America, Spain and the Caribbean. Traditionally, children receive their Christmas presents on this day. In Italy, the kindly witch, La Befana, leaves presents for good children at Epiphany – and a lump of coal for the naughty ones!

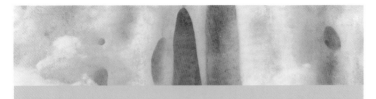

Alicia's Three Kings Festival

'On the day of the Three Kings Festival we ate a special round cake with nuts and fruit. It's supposed to be like Jesus' crown. There's a little toy king hidden inside and my brother found it. At the procession, people were dressed up in amazing costumes. We waved to the Three Kings as they went by. My family held a competition to see how many sweets we could grab – I got ten!'

Alicia, Seville, Spain

In Spain, the Three Kings Festival is colourful and noisy. Huge processions of floats carry people in fancy dress, among them three men dressed up as the Three Kings. The characters on the floats throw out vast quantities of sweets for the crowd. Young and old alike scramble to catch them.

This lucky girl has been chosen to be Mary for this Three Kings Festival in Mexico.

Days to Remember in the USA, January and February

The Americans are proud of their presidents. Since 1971, they have held Presidents' Day on the third Monday of February to celebrate them. On this special holiday, Americans remember great presidents such as George Washington, their very first president (1789–1797), and the 'father of his country'. They honour Abraham Lincoln (US president 1860–1865), who was involved in ending **slavery**.

Martin Luther King (1929–1968) never became president but he was one of the USA's greatest leaders. In the 1950s and 1960s, **African-Americans** did not have the same rights as white people. Martin Luther King led a peaceful movement to try to change the laws to give equal treatment to everybody. Finally, the government began to alter the laws. Tragically, King was murdered by a man who opposed these changes.

This boy is giving a speech to his class about American presidents on Presidents' Day.

Children carrying placards showing Martin Luther King, marching on his special day. The words 'I have a dream' come from a famous speech in which he said he hoped black and white people could live together peacefully one day.

Jia Li's Martin Luther King Day

'At school we talked about how, fifty years ago, black and white kids lived separately and went to different schools. The white kids always had better things. We made up a play about a black child who wanted to drink from a water fountain but some white kids stopped her because it was for whites only. Then we talked about how to treat people fairly and respect people who are different from ourselves.'
Jia Li, Los Angeles, USA

On Martin Luther King Day, the third Monday in January, people study King's life. They join peace parades and march at night with candles. And above all, they try to think about how people from different backgrounds can live peacefully together.

Id ul-Adha

Id ul-Adha means 'feast of the sacrifice'. It's the biggest Muslim festival. Muslims remember when **Allah** commanded the **Prophet** Ibrahim ﷺ to sacrifice his son, Ishmael. This was to test his faith. Ibrahim felt terrible but prepared to do as he was ordered. Yet Allah did not make him kill his son; he provided a lamb to sacrifice instead. Ibrahim had passed the test.

On the day of Id ul-Adha, Muslims get up early. Men and boys say special prayers in the **mosque**; women and girls usually pray at home. Everybody dresses in their finest clothes and gathers for a huge feast with meat.

The meat reminds them of the lamb that was killed instead of Ishmael. The wealthy share their meat with poorer members of the community. People in rich countries send money to poor Muslim countries so that the people there can join in the festivities.

A family dressed in their finest clothes for the festival. In Muslim countries, schools and businesses close for four days so everyone can celebrate.

Osman's Id ul-Adha

'In Turkish we call the celebration *Kurban Bayrami* – it's my favourite festival. We have four days' holiday. On the day of Id, we got up early, showered and put on our best clothes. After morning Id prayers at the mosque, we went to my uncle's big house. We ate tasty beef and rice. Everyone exchanged Id cards, and we kids were given money and presents. Later we visited more relatives.'

Osman, Ankara, Turkey

Id ul-Adha is also a time for praying to Allah for forgiveness. It is an opportunity for forgiving other people for bad things they have done, and making up with them.

Attending prayers at the beautiful mosque of Badshabi in Lahore, Pakistan.

St Valentine's Day, 14 February

Valentine's Day has its origins in the festival of the god Lupercus, back in Roman times. Later, it was adopted by Christians. Valentine was made the patron saint of love.

Hearts and flowers are traditional pictures for Valentine's cards but nowadays cartoon characters appear too.

One story says that Valentine, in prison for his Christian beliefs, fell in love with his jailer's blind daughter. With his love for her and his strong religious faith, he healed her blindness. Before he was taken away to be killed, he wrote her a note. It was signed 'from your Valentine' – the first romantic Valentine's message.

Jen's Valentine's Day

'Mum and I do argue sometimes but on Valentine's Day I made a special effort to show I care about her. I made a card with a big heart on it and I bought her some flowers. Mum was delighted. Then we decided to make Valentine's biscuits. We mixed red food colouring into icing and put a little red heart on each biscuit – very sweet!'

Jen, Bergen, Norway

Nowadays, just before Valentine's Day, the shops are filled with pictures of red hearts, the sign of love. People buy cards to send to their loved one, usually their girlfriend or boyfriend (or sometimes their mum). Some show their love with gifts and flowers too.

Cupid is another symbol for love that appears on cards. He was the cheeky winged child of Venus, Roman goddess of love. According to stories, he fired arrows at people and gods, making them fall head over heels in love.

Designing your own card makes a Valentine's gift more special.

Mahashivaratri, February

Mahashivaratri is a solemn Hindu festival to honour Lord Shiva. To Hindus, he is one of the most important forms of God. Shiva is a symbol of the energy that flows through the world, causing day and night and the pattern of the seasons. Hindus believe there is an everlasting cycle of birth, life, death and new life.

Shiva is sometimes worshipped as the Lord of the Dance. Once a year comes Mahashivaratri, the 'great night of Shiva', when Hindus believe that Shiva performs a special dance. His dancing destroys the old world so that a new one can be born.

A procession in South India to celebrate Mahashivaratri. Shiva is holding a trident, his most powerful weapon.

Hindus visit the temple to watch the *Shiva Linga* being washed with milk.

As it's a solemn festival, people **fast** for the day to clean out their bodies. In the evening they bathe, put on fresh clothes and go to the **mandir** – their temple. They wash a small stone column called a *Shiva Linga* with milk. They perform the **arti** ceremony – moving lamps in circles around the *Shiva Linga* – and sing hymns. Some people stay up all night praying and singing. All this is to honour Shiva.

Prisha's Mahashivaratri

'On Mahashivaratri I went with my family to the *mandir* in the evening. We recited prayers while the *Shiva Linga* was washed with milk. People had brought gifts of food, money and sweets to the temple. They were given out to people like us who haven't got much money so we could enjoy the festival too. I was happy to get some sweets because I don't usually have any!'
Prisha, Maharashtra, India

25

Carnival, February

The roots of carnival go right back to the ancient Greeks and Romans. They celebrated nature springing into life again at the end of winter. Later, in the Middle Ages, carnival became part of the Catholic Christian tradition. In Latin, *carne vale* means 'farewell to meat'. **Catholics** gave up eating meat during **Lent**, the period of forty days before Easter. Carnival was a great opportunity to let go and have a big party before the serious time of Lent began.

A children's group performing at the carnival in Trinidad and Tobago, in the Caribbean islands.

In Catholic countries today, such as in South America and southern Europe, there's a colourful festival parade, with spectacular costumes, live music, dancing and lots of fun out in the streets. The biggest and best known is the carnival in Rio de Janeiro, Brazil.

In France and French-speaking areas, the Mardi Gras season is the ten days before Lent. Mardi Gras means 'fat Tuesday'. People would use up all the rich, fatty foods in the cupboard before Lent. In New Orleans, USA, there's an extravagant street festival with carnival parades through the city.

At the New Orleans Mardi Gras festival, carnival organizations make fantastic costumes and parade through the streets.

Lucas's carnival

'At carnival there's a big competition between the **samba** groups, and special afternoon shows for kids. This year, my neighbourhood had its own *bandas* (say 'bun-dush'), a street carnival. The orchestra led the parade, and there were hundreds of samba dancers in costume. Some wore bathing costumes and a few of the men dressed as women! We soon stopped the traffic and performed a show with cars and buses all around.'

Lucas, Rio de Janeiro, Brazil

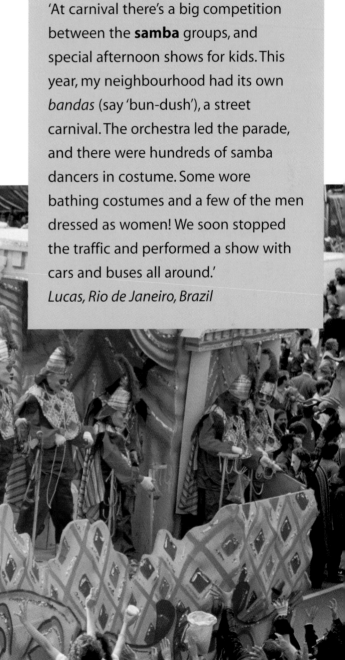

Magha Puja, (February/early March)

At Magha Puja, Buddhists in Thailand remember a significant event in the Buddha's life, which took place three months before the Buddha's death in about 480 BC. Without any warning, 1,250 of his followers came from all different places to see him. The Buddha gave them his most important teachings. He said that people should do good things and try to be kind and generous. They should be patient and never harm living things.

Magha Puja is one of the most important Buddhist celebrations. Followers go to their temple to listen to a talk about the *Dharma*, the Buddhist teachings. As part of their worship they **meditate**, sitting quietly and still with their thoughts.

Buddhists bring offerings of food, fruit or flowers to the temple on festival days.

Rawiwan's Magha Puja

'On Magha Puja, a team from my
school entered a *Dharma* quiz
contest at a Buddhist centre near
Bangkok. We answered questions
about how we should act towards
our family, teachers and Buddhist
community. Out of all the primary
schools, our team won. We were so
happy! We also took part in the
procession around the temple. I
thought about the Buddha and how
to be kind and gentle just like him.'
Rawiwan, Nakhon Pathom, Thailand

These people are lighting candles and incense
sticks at a temple during Magha Puja.

On special holidays, Buddhists do good
actions, such as offering food to monks.
At sunset, they go to the temple and light
candles and incense sticks. Following
prayers, Buddhist monks lead their followers
on a beautiful, silent, candle-lit walk.
Carrying the glowing **incense** sticks and
lighted candles, they walk slowly around
their temple to honour the Buddha. It is
an extremely special, sacred occasion.

29

Calendar of Festivals

Most religions follow a lunar calendar, based on the moon's movements, rather than a solar calendar. They adjust the calendar to keep the festivals in their season. Muslims don't adjust their calendar, so the festivals can be at any time of the year and are not related to the seasons. Sikh festivals are usually three days long because they include the two-day reading of the Sikh holy book before the festival day.

At the time of going to print the dates for Magha Puja for 2005/06 could not be confirmed.

2004

Hanukkah	8–15 December
Christmas	25 December
Kwanzaa	26 December –1 January
New Year celebrations	1 January onwards
Guru Gobind Singh's birthday	3–5 January
Epiphany	6 January
Martin Luther King Day	19 January
Id ul-Adha	2 February
St Valentine's Day	14 February
Presidents' Day	16 February
Mahashivaratri	18 February
Carnival	21–24 February
Magha Puja	5 March

2005

Christmas	25 December
Kwanzaa	26 December– 1 January
Hanukkah	26 December– 2 January
New Year celebrations	1 January onwards
Guru Gobind Singh's birthday	3–5 January
Epiphany	6 January
Martin Luther King Day	17 January
Id ul-Adha	21 January
Carnival	5–8 February
St Valentine's Day	14 February
Presidents' Day	21 February
Mahashivaratri	8 March

2006

Hanukkah	16–24 December
Christmas	25 December
Kwanzaa	26 December – 1 January
New Year celebrations	1 January onwards
Guru Gobind Singh's birthday	3–5 January
Epiphany	6 January
Id ul-Adha	10 January
Martin Luther King Day	16 January
St Valentine's Day	14 February
Presidents' Day	20 February
Carnival	25–28 February
Mahashivaratri	26 February

Glossary

Advent The four-week time of preparation just before Christmas.

African-American An American whose family came from Africa long ago.

Allah The Muslim name for God.

ancestors The people in a person's family who lived long ago are his or her ancestors.

arti Lighting candles and moving them in a circle in front of images of gods, to honour them.

Catholics Members of the Roman Catholic Church, which is led by the Pope, or Holy Father.

cornmeal Flour made from maize.

fast To go without food for religious reasons, or to eat only certain foods – as Hindus do.

gurdwara The building where Sikhs go to meet and worship.

gurpurb A special day to remember the birth or death of one of the ten Sikh Gurus.

Guru A holy Buddhist or Sikh teacher.

harmonium A musical instrument like a small organ.

Lent The season of forty days before Easter. Some Christians give up foods or activities they enjoy, to help them to remember Jesus' suffering.

incense sticks Sticks that are burnt to make a nice smell. They are often used in religious ceremonies.

mandir A place of worship for Hindus, also called a temple.

martial arts Any of the fighting sports that include judo and karate.

mass A service in which bread and wine are used to help people to remember Jesus.

meditate To sit quietly and still with your thoughts to help you to become calm, content and wise.

mosque The place where Muslims meet, pray and study.

northern hemisphere The northern half of the Earth.

Orthodox Churches Churches such as the Russian Church and the Greek Church, sometimes called the Eastern Churches.

Prophet For Muslims, one of the special messengers who brought God's message to the world.

samba A dance from Brazil.

slavery Owning people and forcing them to work for their owner. Slavery ended in the USA in 1864.

southern hemisphere The southern half of the Earth.

tabla drums A pair of small Indian drums that are played with the hands.

tropical Countries that are tropical are in the tropics, the hottest area of the world. This area is above and below the Equator, an imaginary line drawn around the middle of the Earth.

unity Being in agreement and working together.

Further Information

Books for Children

Celebrate Buddhist Festivals by Clive and Jane Erricker (Heinemann Library, 1996)

Celebrate Christian Festivals by Jan Thompson (Heinemann Library, 1996)

Celebrate Hindu Festivals by Dilip Kadodwala, Paul Gateshill (Heinemann Library, 1996)

Celebrate Islamic Festivals by Khadijah Knight (Heinemann Library, 1996)

Celebrate Jewish Festivals by Angela Wood (Heinemann Library, 1996)

Celebrate Sikh Festivals by John Coutts (Heinemann Library, 1996)

My Buddhist Year, My Christian Year, My Hindu Year, My Jewish Year, My Muslim Year, My Sikh Year, all by Cath Senker (Hodder Wayland, 2002-2003)

Websites

www.theresite.org.uk/
UK site with RE resources and links.

website.lineone.net/~jlancs/startpage.htm
Schoolchildren from Frenchwood school talk about their religions, including festivals: Hindu, Muslim, Buddhist and Christian faiths.

Index

All numbers in **bold** refer to pictures as well as text.